WILD ANIMAL BABIES

BEAR CUBS

NOAH RICCARDI

PowerKiDS press

Published in 2027 by The Rosen Publishing Group, Inc.
2544 Clinton Street, Buffalo, NY 14224

First Edition

Book Design: Marley Richmond

Photo Credits: Cover, pp. 1, 19 Giedriius/Shutterstock.com; p. 5 evaurban/Shutterstock.com; p. 7 AB Photographie/Shutterstock.com; p. 9 Alec Taylor/Shutterstock.com; p. 11 Danny Ye/Shutterstock.com; p. 13 Anne Kiel/Shutterstock.com; p. 15 Volodymyr Burdiak/Shutterstock.com; p. 17 knelson20/Shutterstock.com; p. 21 Tony Campbell/Shutterstock.com.

Cataloging-in-Publication Data
Names: Riccardi, Noah.
Title: Bear Cubs / Noah Riccardi.
Description: Buffalo, New York : PowerKids Press, 2027. | Series: Wild animal babies | Includes glossary and index.
Identifiers: ISBN 9781538295397 (pbk.) | ISBN 9781538295403 (library bound) | ISBN 9781538295410 (ebook)
Subjects: LCSH: Bear cubs--Juvenile literature. | Forest animals--Infancy--Juvenile literature.
Classification: LCC QL737.C27 R533 2027 | DDC 599.781392--dc23

Manufactured in China

CPSIA Compliance Information: Batch #QS27PK. For Further Information contact Rosen Publishing, at 1-800-237-9932.

CONTENTS

Bears Around the World

Bears are **mammals**. There are many kinds of bears around the world. Polar bears live in the freezing **Arctic**. Sun bears live in tropical forests. A baby bear is called a cub.

A Bear Is Born

A mother bear gives birth to her cubs. She can have one to four cubs at a time. But she usually has twins. Newborn cubs are very small. They **nurse** to survive.

Different kinds of bears are born at certain times of year. Giant pandas are born in the fall. Black bears and polar bears are born in the winter. Sun bears can be born any time of the year.

Baby Bears

Newborn cubs are very small. Black bear cubs weigh less than 0.5 pounds (0.2 kg) and are **bald**. Newborn pandas weigh about 4 ounces (113 g) and are blind. Baby cubs need their mother for warmth and food.

Cubs grow very quickly. Polar bears can grow to more than 20 pounds (9 kg) in three months. Black bears can weigh 80 pounds (36 kg) by their first birthday. Cubs need to grow quickly to get ready for the wild.

Life in the Den

Newborn cubs live with their mothers in small homes called dens. Black bears and giant pandas use **hollow** tree trunks as dens. Polar bears use **snowdrifts** for dens. Grizzly bears in Alaska dig dens into hills.

Cubs live in the den for around three months. They spend this time nursing and growing. Bear cubs learn to walk in the den. When they grow big enough, cubs are ready to leave the den.

Leaving the Den

Cubs leave the den with their mother. The cubs are strong and can eat **solid food** now. They still nurse from their mother, too. Their mother **defends** her cubs in the wild.

On Their Own

Cubs stay with their mothers until they can survive on their own. This usually happens between 18 and 36 months old. Then cubs leave their mother and live alone.

GLOSSARY

Arctic: The northernmost part of Earth.

bald: Without any fur or hair.

defends: Protects from danger.

hollow: Empty in the middle.

mammals: Animals that have hair or fur and that feed milk to their babies.

nurse: To drink milk from the mother's body.

snowdrifts: Piles of snow that build up in the winter.

solid food: Food that needs to be chewed.

FOR MORE INFORMATION

BOOKS

Ali, Nadia. *Animals Live in Homes*. North Mankato, MN: Capstone Publishing, 2023.

Andrews, Elizabeth. *Bears*. Minneapolis, MN: Abdo Publishing, 2023.

WEBSITES

Britannica Kids: Bear
kids.britannica.com/kids/article/bear/352836
Learn more about bears at this website.

National Geographic Kids: Black Bear
kids.nationalgeographic.com/animals/mammals/facts/black-bear
Learn about the American black bear at this site.

Publisher's note to educators and parents: Our editors have carefully reviewed these websites to ensure that they are suitable for students. Many websites change frequently, however, and we cannot guarantee that a site's future contents will continue to meet our high standards of quality and educational value. Be advised that students should be closely supervised whenever they access the internet.

INDEX